10 CHRISTMAS DUETS VOL 1.

CONTENTS

Jingle Bells

James Pierpont

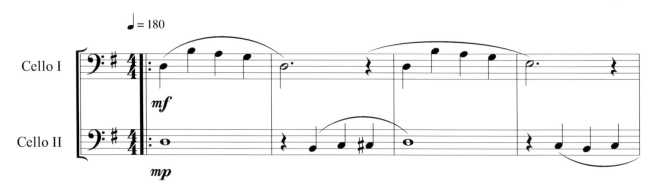

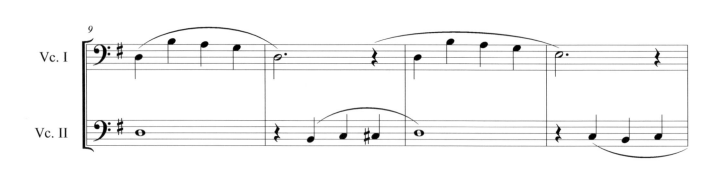

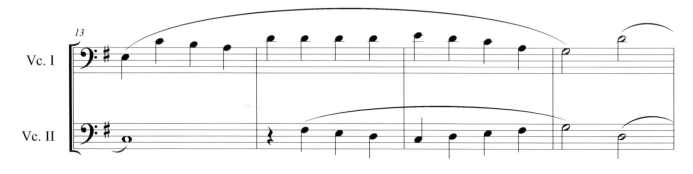

Jingle Bells

Silent Night

Franz Gruber

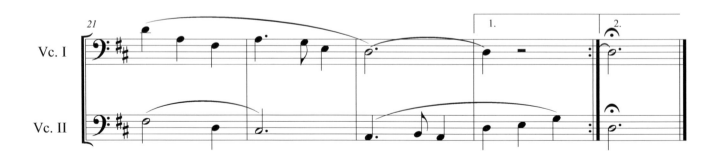

What Child Is This
(Greensleeves)

Traditional

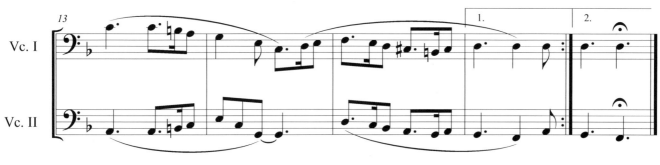

O Come All Ye Faithful

John Francis Wade

Joy To The World

Handel

Away in a Manger

James R. Murray

We Three Kings

John Henry Hopkins, Jr.

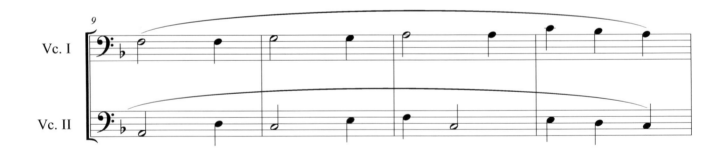

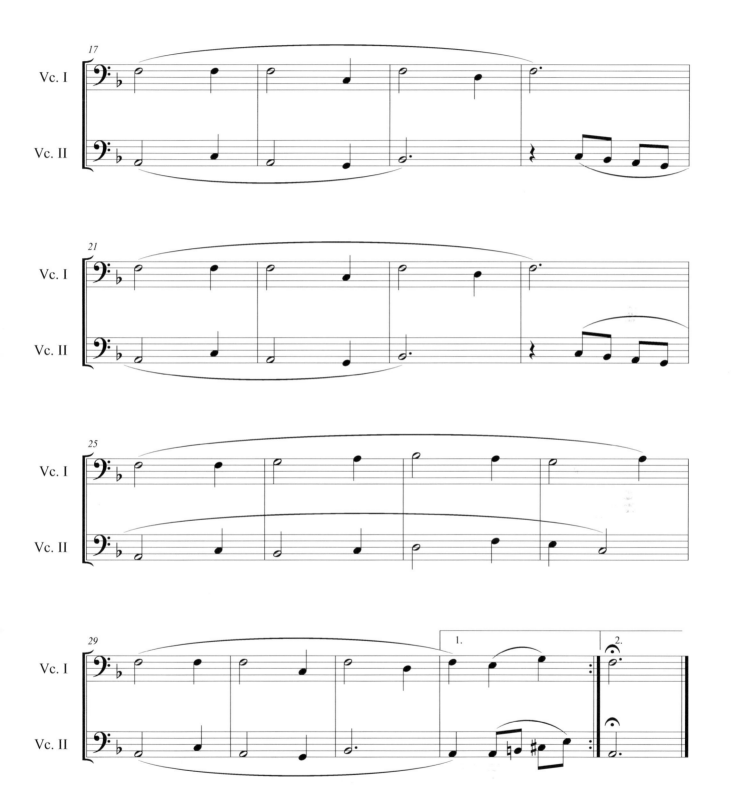

Away in a Manger
(Cradle Song)

William J. Kirkpatrick

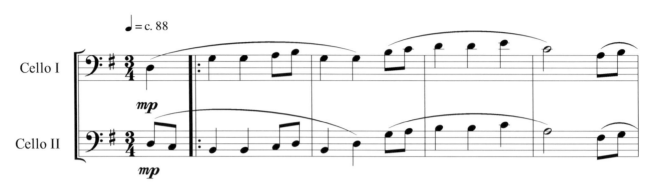

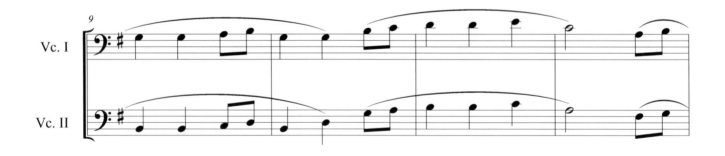

O Holy Night

Adolphe Adam

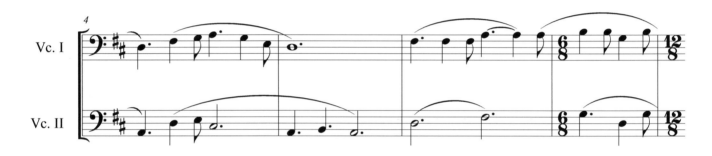

O Holy Night

The First Noel

Traditional

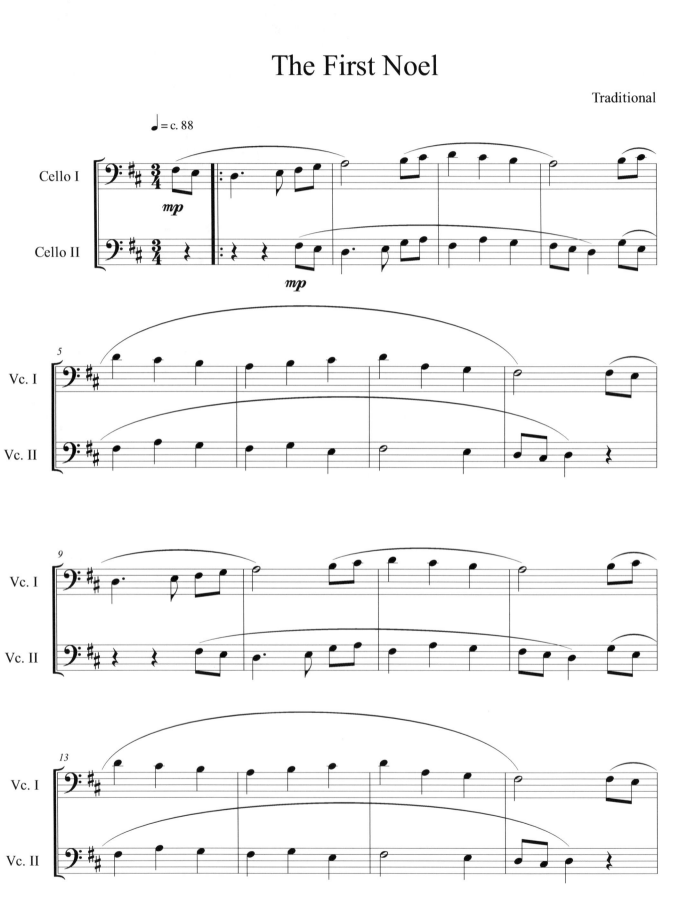

Jingle Bells

Cello 1

James Pierpont

Jingle Bells

Cello 2

James Pierpont

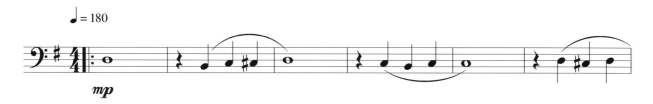

Silent Night

Cello 2

Franz Gruber

Silent Night

Cello 1

Franz Gruber

What Child Is This
(Greensleeves)

Cello 1

Traditional

What Child Is This
(Greensleeves)

Cello 2

Traditional

O Come All Ye Faithful

Cello 1

John Francis Wade

O Come All Ye Faithful

Cello 2

John Francis Wade

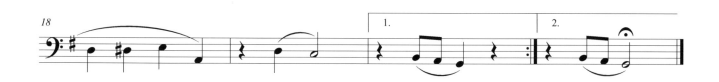

Joy To The World

Cello 1

Handel

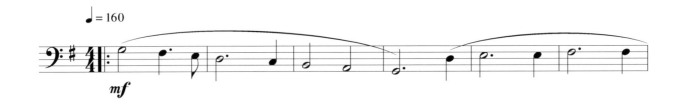

Joy To The World

Cello 2

Handel

Away in a Manger

Cello 1

James R. Murray

Away in a Manger

Cello 2

James R. Murray

We Three Kings

Cello 1

John Henry Hopkins, Jr.

We Three Kings

Cello 2

John Henry Hopkins, Jr.

Away in a Manger
(Cradle Song)

Cello 1

William J. Kirkpatrick

Away in a Manger
(Cradle Song)

Cello 2

William J. Kirkpatrick

O Holy Night

Cello 1

Adolphe Adam

O Holy Night

Cello 2

Adolphe Adam

The First Noel

Cello 2

Traditional

The First Noel

Cello 1

Traditional

Made in the USA
Las Vegas, NV
07 November 2023

80421813R00022